C000064941

Addicted to
Hope

A Handbook for Discovering Hope in a Hopeless World

By
Penelope Rivera
Licensed Professional Counselor
Ordained Minister

Trilogy Christian Publishers

A Wholly Owned Subsidiary of Trinity Broadcasting Network

2442 Michelle Drive

Tustin, CA 92780

Addicted to Hope: A Handbook for Discovering Hope in a Hopeless World

Copyright © 2023 Penelope Rivera

All Scripture quotations, unless otherwise noted, taken from THE HOLY BIBLE, NEW INTERNATIONAL VERSION®, NIV® Copyright © 1973, 1978, 1984, 2011 by Biblica, Inc.® Used by permission. All rights reserved worldwide.

Scripture quotations marked MSG are taken from *THE MESSAGE,* copyright (c) 1993, 2002, 2018 by Eugene H. Peterson. Used by permission of NavPress. All rights reserved. Represented by Tyndale House Publishers, Inc.

Scripture quotations marked ESV are taken from the ESV® Bible (The Holy Bible, English Standard Version®), copyright © 2001 by Crossway Bibles, a publishing ministry of Good News Publishers. Used by permission. All rights reserved.

All rights reserved, including the right to reproduce this book or portions thereof in any form whatsoever.

For information, address Trilogy Christian Publishing

Rights Department, 2442 Michelle Drive, Tustin, Ca 92780.

Trilogy Christian Publishing/ TBN and colophon are trademarks of Trinity Broadcasting Network.

For information about special discounts for bulk purchases, please contact Trilogy Christian Publishing.

Manufactured in the United States of America

Trilogy Disclaimer: The views and content expressed in this book are those of the author and may not necessarily reflect the views and doctrine of Trilogy Christian Publishing or the Trinity Broadcasting Network.

10 9 8 7 6 5 4 3 2 1

Library of Congress Cataloging-in-Publication Data is available.

ISBN 979-8-88738-270-8

ISBN 979-8-88738-271-5 (ebook)

Dedication

This book is dedicated to my family, close friends, and counselor who unwaveringly stood by me during intense times in my life believing with me for miracles that made no sense. I am grateful for their addiction to hope that enabled them to believe along with me and encourage me when I wanted to give up. I am especially thankful for my dad, who is one of the most hope addicted person's I know. I can call him at any time of the day or night, and he is always there to encourage me and direct me back to faith and hope. Most of all, I am thankful for my Lord and Savior, Jesus Christ. Without my relationship with Christ, there would be no hope. I have seen God show up in my life countless times, and He continues to do so every day.

Contents

Introduction

I have been a Licensed Professional Counselor for over eighteen years. I have the privilege and honor to sit with people every day and walk through the dark valleys in their lives and assist them in developing their addiction to hope.

I sat with a 15-year-old male client in my office and he said to me, "I just want to have hope." Those words struck deep inside of me. Here in front of me was a 15-year-old boy who didn't have hope and was searching for it. The world is full of people, young and old, searching for hope.

Hope is an essential ingredient for life. It is when a person feels hopeless they become depressed, despondent, and oftentimes suicidal. Without hope, life becomes meaningless. I have many individuals come into my office, expressing feelings of hopelessness and despair, looking for hope.

My desire is to help people find hope and become addicted to it.

Below is part of my journal entries I had written during a time in my life where I was fighting for my addiction to hope. As you read it, some of you may feel validated and comforted by the raw emotions and thoughts you may experience during your own battle of your addiction to hope.

Is faith and hope believing in something that defies what you see in the natural?

Is it believing what God has spoken to you even when the things around you say otherwise?

Is it trusting in what you know God has spoken to you when all hell rises against it, trying to convince you otherwise?

It looks impossible. But isn't that the purpose of faith?

To cause the impossible to become possible?

Is the very essence of faith believing that God is so powerful and has the ability to answer a prayer and do something that defies all rationale?

Isn't faith looking in the face of doubt and calling it a liar?

It's easier to give up than to have faith.

I cannot see the evidence in the natural realm; therefore, faith is necessary in order to rely on what is happening in the spiritual realm that I cannot see.

I sound crazy speaking things into existence that are not. Faith isn't logical. It doesn't make sense. Faith defies logic. It has to, otherwise I would not need it.

Nothing is making sense to me. The only logical thought is to give up and retreat. Even that doesn't make sense to me. When hope takes a hold of your heart, all you can do is grab a hold of it and keep pushing forward.

Giving up seems like a viable option, but faith will not let me give up nor give in. My heart, at times, fails and sinks beneath the weight of discouragement. But faith is like the buoy that floats me back up to the top. I can't stay under the weight. Faith lifts me and holds me steady. I don't like it at times, but it won't let me give up. It brings hope when everything seems hopeless. When everything logical around me says there is no hope, faith comes with an expectation that God is able. God will do what He says. Nothing can stop God.

It feels like an obsession. I can't let go. I can't stop praying and believing and speaking it. My mind will not move off declaring what God is speaking to me. I don't have to understand it; I just have to believe it. Preparing for disappointment is not faith. In this very moment, God is orchestrating events, and He is orchestrating things in the supernatural and physical realm that I cannot see that are in the preparation for the desires of my heart to be complete and fulfilled.

I cannot ride the waves of emotions when I am walking with faith and hope. It feels like a whirlpool. I have to be willing to swim with the current to break out of it and see the results.

Everything in the natural is telling me to give up. I need to give it up and let go. But something in my spirit won't let me walk away.

Faith is blind. I don't like it. I can't see, but yet I have to believe in what I can't see. Hope deferred makes the heart sick. I feel sick. I want to let go, but I can't. Am I crazy?

Faith is believing in something when people around you do not. Faith is not reliant on those around you who don't believe. I cannot base my faith on what those around me believe or do not believe.

People will try to talk you out of speaking with faith. When you speak things that are not as though they are, some people will try to pull you back into what you can see, which is not faith.

Faith is looking to what will be, not at what is now. No matter what I see or don't see, I will still believe.

Faith is producing fruit even though we can't see it at the time it's being produced. It is like the fruit tree. The fruit tree starts to bud and grow fruit that you don't see until the appointed time.

God will not contradict what He says. It doesn't matter if the devil does not want the promise to happen. He can't see what God is doing, and he does not have the authority to prevent it from happening.

There's an overwhelming push to get me to give up. Let go. But I can't. Faith will not allow me to throw in the towel. My flesh wants to retreat, but my spirit takes over. The constant worship I've been doing has equipped my spiritual person to overthrow my physical being. So I will pray that much harder.

I don't see anything. It makes me want to dig my heels deeper. I will not stop. I feel a stubborn wave come over me. Doubt will not win. Faith will be the victor!

I hear the fiery darts hitting my shield of faith. I smell the smoke as they are extinguished by my faith-soaked shield. They keep coming.

My shield is steady.

It's dark. I can't see. The only thing I can see is the light of my faith. When will I see further ahead? Right now, I can only see one step in front of me.

The enemy keeps attacking me with my own logic; how I think. My own distorted beliefs that I've set up for so many years. God, let your voice and my faith yell above the noise, so all I hear is you!

When does God ever operate through logic?

Victory must be near. The battle has intensified. I'm tired. The fiery darts don't stop. Lord, help me hang on to my faith. I don't want to quit. It's too close. The enemy mocks and antagonizes me, telling me to give up. Telling me it won't happen. SHUT UP!

Praise. All I can do is praise.

Praise... worship... praise.

Waves of peace and calm flow over me.

Turbulent waves of doubt come up out of nowhere, but God's peace quickly overpowers it.

The evidence of my faith will soon arrive.

The enemy is still in hot pursuit. Praise... worship... my praise and worship just launched a grenade at the enemy. He doesn't stand a chance. God to my rescue. My faith will stand.

Again? It's bleak. It's so dark. I've been hit in a familiar place. Distorted beliefs I thought I had eradicated are creeping back.

The battle has intensified. I must be close to victory, even though it looks like it is nowhere near. God, let my faith stay strong.

The Spirit is saying pull from within. Pull from within what I have taught you and what I have placed inside of you. You have the words, and you have the power in you because greater is He that is in you than he that is in the world.

You have equipped me. You have prepared me. I will stand on Your word, for Your Word is life and truth. The enemy cannot steal what you have purposed and planned.

Faith is blind. I don't like it. It causes me to go deeper. To trust at a deeper level. Even though I can't see it, I still believe.

No weapon formed against me will stand. Not even a weapon that for years would knock me out.

Don't give up.

The enemy got close. All I hear is him taunting, accusing. My heart is failing. Please rescue me!

I don't understand. It looks as if what I'm praying for is hopeless. Victory must be close. Don't quit! It's so hard. New reasons pop up as to why I should quit. They make sense. But I know what God has told me to do. Obedience is better than sacrifice.

I hit rock bottom today. It was awful. Part of me felt an eerie sense of calm going back to the place I had lived for so long. The other part of me felt sick, and I did not want to stay there. Immediately, I cried out to God. I don't want to walk without hope and faith any longer. Returning to the old place was not comforting. It was actually very frightening. It made me sick to my stomach. It was a place of no hope. I felt separated from you, God. I immediately cried for help. God immediately lifted me up out of the pit. I can't go back there.

Thank you, God, for the people you send to intercede for me. I will rise. I will continue to walk in faith and hope! The old, distorted patterns and thinking are no longer my place of safety or comfort.

Faith is now my new home and is now my safe place. It's completely dark. It's eerily silent. This is when faith must rise. I'm not called to understand the silence and the darkness. I'm only called to pray and believe. It is still dark and eerily silent. Pray and believe.

Thank you for the glimpse of light. A special gift. Even when I am faithless, You remain faithful. You are so good to me.

The enemy wants to twist and distort the gift You gave me. Block him. Destroy him. Preserve the gift in me.

An interesting sense of calm... an assurance. I've never been here before. I'm not sure what to do. Lord, guide me. Teach me. It's a new place.

The old patterns want to come back in. Even when I entertain the old, distorted thoughts, they have no power. It's as if the old me wants to bring them into a position of power again, but the faith within me does not allow them to take residence.

Victory is so close I feel like I can almost reach out and grab it.

The very thing God is helping me and teaching me at this time is to trust Him with my heart. He would not bring me this far to take away what I have been praying and believing for because it would negate the very purpose of why I'm going through his journey of faith.

If I can imagine the good things that will happen, just think how much more God will do. He says He will do exceedingly, abundantly, far above what I can think or imagine. I'm excited to see what God has in store!

Hope is not striving for something. Hope is praying and believing and releasing to God. I have now released this to God, and I will no longer strive in my own strength. It is peaceful. I now can focus on the goodness of God and the faithfulness of God, trusting He will bring what has been prayed and believed for in faith and hope will take place.

I'm exhausted trying to earn God's goodness and blessings He has for me. I don't have to earn God's goodness. He wants to give me good things just because He loves me. I will never be able to earn or work for anything God has for me. I don't need to. It's a restful place.

Why? Why can't I just trust? Why does this spirit of fear keep attacking me? Why is it still silent? Why can't I stay consistently strong in faith? I am so weary. How close is victory? Please God. Give me a sign.

My heart is faint. The silence does not mean it won't happen. Silence does not equal no.

The devil has waged a psychological, spiritual attack. Fighting for faith and hope is combatting every distorted belief and thought that has taken root in your

mind. It's exhausting.

I'm expecting a miracle.

I'm expecting God's promises.

I will see a victory.

I just literally saw God take the mountain and turn it into a smooth plain right before my eyes! The miracle is here! I have seen a victory! Hebrews 11:6, "But without faith it is impossible to please Him, for he who comes to God must believe that He is, AND that *He is a rewarder of those who diligently seek Him"* (NKJV).

God loves me so much that He rewarded my

faith. Hope and victory are here!

My desire for you as you read this book is that you become addicted to hope and that you experience the wonderful promises God has for your life.

Addicted to Hope

You may be wondering, what does it mean to be addicted to hope? I will first define what it is to have an addiction. An addiction can be described as a strong inclination to do, use, or indulge in something repeatedly. I'm sure you can relate since everyone on some level has something we might say we are addicted to, whether it is coffee, soda, chocolate (that's mine!), certain foods, exercise, etc. Some of you may have struggled with a serious addiction, such as alcohol, drugs, sex, or gambling. We all can understand the concept of being addicted to something.

Addicted to hope is having a strong belief in something that seems impossible, yet you are unable to stop hoping for and having an expectancy that something will happen. You can't stop believing. An addiction to hope is tied to an expectancy. You have a strong inclination or an urge to believe in the impossible. It goes against our natural way of thinking. Our human nature typically leans to the negative. Our human emotions are fluid and can change on a whim. When we are faced with a situation that seems impossible, without an addiction to hope, we begin to vacillate and easily lose hope, leading to discouragement.

The Bible encourages us to have an addiction to hope. Romans 15:13 states, "May the God of hope fill you with all joy and peace as you trust in him, so that you may *overflow with hope* by the power of the Holy Spirit." This is the hope that goes beyond our human capacity and ability. Hebrews 6:19 states, "We who have run for our very lives to God have every reason to grab the promised hope with both hands and never let go. It's an unbreakable spiritual lifeline reaching past all appearances right to the very presence of God" (Message Bible). This is the perfect example of an addiction to hope! Are you grabbing hold of the promised hope with both hands and never letting go?

Our addiction to hope comes from a relationship with God and it comes from God. However, not everyone who has a relationship with God has an addiction to hope. As you read this book, you will see how your relationship with Christ is relevant and crucial to developing and maintaining an addiction to hope. If you do not have a relationship with Christ, it is very simple to start one. All it takes is a simple prayer such as this:

> Dear God, I know I'm a sinner, and I ask for your forgiveness. I believe Jesus Christ is Your Son. I believe that He died for my sin and that you raised Him to life. I want to trust Him as my Savior and follow Him as Lord, from this day forward. Guide my life and help me to do your will. I pray this in the name of Jesus. Amen.
>
> (Prayer by Billy Graham.)[1]

God desires and longs for us to become addicted to the hope only He can give!

As I was writing this book, I was in the middle of another battle for my own addiction to hope. I had been praying and believing for ten months for something I knew God directed and confirmed to me multiple times. However, I received a notification that I interpreted as all hope is gone. It isn't going to happen. Yes, I have to admit I was thrown for a loop. I knew what God had told me during those ten months. I had been exercising my faith and speaking affirmations over my situation for ten months, and I believed it was coming to a successful end soon. When I got word that all hope for that to happen was gone, it felt devastating. I don't like to admit it, but I cycled down, deep down. I hit the bottom hard. I couldn't understand why this happened when I was so sure things were going to turn around. I had even confessed that a breakthrough was coming soon! It had to! After all, God's word for me for that year was New Year's Redemption and God had already done some incredible things in me throughout that crazy year. I just knew that the promise would be fulfilled by the end of the year, or at least be well on its way.

What happened to me? Where was my addiction to hope? Why didn't I get up immediately and start confessing how great my God is, and how my God is a mountain mover, and He is a way-maker? You might be asking if I have an addiction to hope, why did I start faltering? First of all, I am human. And there will always be something that will contend for your addiction to hope. I also did something many people do when they begin a battle for their addiction to hope and, in that moment, we may not realize what we are doing is counterproductive to our addiction to hope. I began to suppress my addiction to hope. The stronger your addiction to hope, the stronger the battle will be to maintain it. This battle was over the desires of my heart. This is why the fear became so intense and I became susceptible to discouragement.

How does the devil war against us? Through fear. The opposite of faith is fear. When I thought what I had been praying and believing for was not going to come to pass (however, God is still in control), I allowed fear to sweep over me. You will notice as you read through this book that fear is one of the major tactics that will be used against you with every battle you face for your addiction to hope. I started to allow fear to talk to me. That was my first mistake. I was ready to give up. I was ready to end my addiction to hope. In fact, I said to God, "well, this ended my addiction to hope." I'm sure you have been there before. I am sure there has been something in your life you jumped all in and were believing for, only to receive a notification that it isn't going to happen.

When I went to sleep that night, fear kept talking, and I kept listening. In fact, I started having a conversation with fear. Another big mistake. I started fearing that everything I believed about God and His promises was a lie. I don't like to admit it, but those thoughts entered my mind. Like I said earlier, I hit the bottom hard. It scared me that those thoughts were even entering my mind. I knew I had drawn closer to God than I had ever been during the past ten months and it alarmed me to think, was it all a lie? I was trying to figure out where I went wrong. I was angry at my addiction to hope. I was sure this addiction had misled me to believe in something that was never going to happen.

I immediately felt foolish for believing in the impossible. I started thinking of all the judgments people would make. My therapist's mind condemned me for believing in something that didn't make sense. Thoughts of the past, when I had prayed and believed and I didn't get the answer I expected, were swirling in my head. Satan was waging a psychological, spiritual warfare against me and he was using a familiar weapon against me. Fear.

In your battle for your addiction to hope, it is important to understand that fear is the enemy of rest. In order to fight a battle well, you need to be well-rested. Have you noticed that when you are worried and/or anxious about something, you cannot sleep? Fear works on the mind being at a disadvantage. When you do not sleep well or at all, your thoughts become distorted. When you are physically tired, you are more likely to listen to fear and accept it as truth. Fear works off of distorted beliefs that have already been established in your belief system. What does that mean? One of the thoughts that was swirling in my head was a distorted belief that God does not care about the desires of my heart. This belief creates an immense amount of anxiety and fear for me. Why? Because this belief is based on a lie. Truth does not bring about fear and anxiety. Truth brings peace.

This distorted belief had been established years earlier in my life. I became triggered when I allowed this fear a seat at my table, and I was conversing with it once again. I think I was most disappointed in myself for opening the door to that fear, because God had been doing a work in me over the past several years to break this distorted belief. This was a sign I had not yet conquered this lie. Maybe you have a fear that you have struggled with for years that has created a distorted belief about God and attempts to keep you from being addicted to hope.

Something important we need to be aware of is that we have an enemy, an adversary, Satan, who hates our addiction to hope. This is one addiction he does not want us to have. He will do anything to break your addiction to hope. Fear is a tactic he uses frequently to discourage the beginning of any addiction to hope or break your current addiction to hope. I felt it. The first thing Satan does when he wants to break your addiction to hope is to cause you to question who God is and to cause you to doubt God's love for you. It bothered me that I fell prey to Satan's tactic to break my addiction to hope.

Did I give up my addiction to hope? No. God comes through when the enemy comes in. I'm thankful God fights my battles for me. Isaiah 54:17 tells us that no weapon formed against us will prosper and every word spoken against us in judgment we will condemn, for this is the heritage we have as servants of the Lord (paraphrase).

The next morning, God came to my rescue. He wasn't going to allow me to stay defeated, and I wasn't willing to stay defeated, because God had developed an addiction to hope in me earlier in my life. God's hope is "an unbreakable spiritual lifeline reaching past all appearances right to the very presence of God!" (Hebrews 6:19, MSG). The next morning, as I opened up my social media, there was a notification from one of the pastors I follow online. The sermon for that day was exactly what I needed to hear to reignite my addiction to hope. When you have developed an addiction to hope, God will not allow the enemy to steal it. Even though my circumstances did not change in that moment, I am addicted to hope and even when all may seem lost, there is still a stubborn desire to hope and believe, because my hope is not in a person or a thing. My hope is in God.

I do not think it is a coincidence that while I was writing this book, the biggest battle for my addiction to hope was being challenged. If I can be convinced to let go of my addiction to hope in the most significant area of my life, this book will not be finished. The last thing the enemy wants you and me to have is an addiction to hope, because he will not be able to defeat us. It creates "an unbreakable spiritual lifeline" between you and God where the impossible becomes possible.

Developing an Addiction to Hope

You might be wondering how you develop an addiction to hope? What I have found in my life and the lives of many of my clients is that the process of developing an addiction to hope begins in the midst of dark times in your life. In Hosea 2:15, God is talking to the children of Israel, and He says He will "make the Valley of [Trouble] a door of hope." I love that. Your Valley of Trouble is your door to hope! In this chapter, I am going to be transparent about some very dark times in my life that became the door for God to develop and foster my addiction to hope. The Bible says (1 Kings 8:12) God dwells in thick darkness. I am so thankful that God came and dwelled with me during the times of thick darkness in my life.

It was the year 2000, a few years before my son was born. I was teaching kindergarten full time and going to school full time for my master's degree. In the meantime, I was still heavily involved in ministry at my church. I was actively involved on the worship team, leading a weekly addictions group, and teaching a class on Sunday mornings. I was burning the candle at both ends. Let's not forget about the homework and tests! I was not eating well, and I did not have a healthy sleep routine.

It was during this time I started having random panic attacks. It started with one or two a week. Then it progressed to daily panic attacks, and then to several times a day. It quickly progressed to me being in a state of non-stop panic. The panic attacks could happen while I was driving, sitting at home, school, at work teaching, and while I was at church. I could not go anywhere without having a panic attack. I had dealt with anxiety since I was a child, but this was something completely different. I felt like I was going insane. I didn't know what was happening to my mind and my body. I felt out of control. It was a hopeless feeling. I ended up seeing my doctor, who determined I had pushed my body to its limit. I had started having issues with my blood sugar since I had not been eating properly, which resulted in the random panic attacks. He recommended I start taking an anti-anxiety medication. At that time, I did not know or fully understand the medication, so I refused and was determined to do it on my own.

This was a very dark time for me. I spent a lot of time in my closet crying uncontrollably. I would call my dad and he would pray for me and encourage me. I had a fear of leaving my house, afraid I would have a panic attack wherever I would go. I could barely make it through my day at work. Since my husband was detached from his emotions, he was not able to support me during this time.

It was during this very dark time in my life that God began to develop in me an addiction to hope. All I could do was cling to God. I couldn't function without Him. The first step in developing an addiction to hope is being in a place where all you can do is cling to God. You have nothing else. Ephesian 1:18, 19 says, "I pray that the eyes of your heart may be enlightened in order that you may know the hope to which he has called you, the riches of his glorious inheritance in his holy people, and his incomparably great power for us who believe." It is during the dark times we become enlightened that we need hope and the hope God has called us to. It isn't a natural hope. It is a hope that is only found in God's "glorious inheritance" and in "his incomparably great power for us who believe!" There are riches, a great inheritance, and a power that comes from an addiction to hope because an addiction to hope is founded in the very being of who God is, not in our humanity. It is during the dark times that we become enlightened to our need for divine hope.

The only way I was able to get through each day was to read three to four times a day Psalm 91, Psalm 40, and Psalm 41. It was the first thing I would do in the morning before getting out of bed. I would read them during my lunch hour. I would read them in the evening after dinner and always before bed. In the evening, I would turn on the television to help distract me from the crazy thoughts and panic feeling. It seemed like every channel I turned to Paula White-Cain would be preaching. It is important to understand that God will use key people during your darkest moments to help develop and foster in you an addiction to hope. It may be a friend, counselor, pastor, or a family member. These key people will bring hope to you, encourage you in the Word of God, and many times will give you a word from God to help lift you up. Every time I heard Paula White speak and/or preach, hope was being developed inside of me. She spoke with words of power and authority that only come from God.

It was not only hope rising inside of me but also a power that was rising up within me. It was that power I mentioned earlier in Ephesians chapter one. I began to speak over me the scriptures I was reading three to four times a day. I ended up memorizing them. I would declare God's truth and hope in my life to combat the fear. We have to remember fear is a tactic the enemy uses to prevent us from developing an addiction to hope or to break our current addiction to hope. But our God is stronger than any spirit of fear! Romans 8:37 says, "Yet in all these things we are more than conquerors through Him who loved us." We are more than conquerors! That means we do not only conquer the fear, but we take over the territory and everything around it! It is important to have a full understanding that God will cause us to become more than a conqueror.

Many times, I would wake up at two or three in the morning in a state of panic. I would go downstairs with my Bible to read and speak out loud scriptures on peace. I would pray the scriptures and with the authority God has given each of us through Christ, I would command the fear to go. I marked and highlighted multiple scriptures on peace throughout my Bible in order to reference them quickly. I never knew when I was going to need to access them.

One of my favorite scriptures that became very important to me during this time is 2 Timothy 1:7, "For God has not given us a spirit of fear, but of power and of love and of a sound mind" (NKJV). During this time, I did not feel like I had a sound mind. The fear and panic caused me to feel like I was crazy.

As I began to use these scriptures multiple times a day, hope began to rise in me. I can't explain it. All I know is that God gave me the power, and He began to instill into my life the hope only He can bring. I would like to say everything changed overnight or within a few months. But it didn't. It was about a year before the panic disorder was completely gone. I struggled with some of the lingering fearful thoughts, but they soon disappeared. My addiction to hope was developed. Once you allow God to develop an addiction to hope in you, He will continue to foster it. As with all addictions, they become stronger and stronger the more you engage in it. It didn't stop there with me. I didn't want it to stop. It had forever changed me.

I compare developing an addiction to hope with exercising. I love to workout. I have worked out for years and I enjoy it. I have learned that in order to keep building muscle mass and maintain it, I need to continue working out consistently and I need to continue to challenge my muscles with heavier weights and more difficult exercises. If I stop working out for six to nine months, my body is not going to maintain the muscle I have developed. It is the same with an addiction to hope. You have to use it to maintain it. Trust me, there will be plenty of opportunities in your life to use and maintain your addiction to hope if you don't allow fear to stop it.

After the panic disorder, I walked through another dark time in my life. I was five months pregnant with my son when my mom was diagnosed with stage four colon cancer. It was devastating. I was going through one of the most joyous times of my life and one of the most difficult times of my life at the same time. The doctors weren't sure my mom would live six months from the date of her diagnosis. However, God intervened.

A month before my son was born, my mom seemed to be doing better, and she looked better than she had in years. We were all very hopeful and believed that God had healed her. My mom was able to be there for the birth of my son. It seemed as if all was going well.

A month after my son was born, my mom's health began to deteriorate quickly. It was all happening so fast it was hard to process what was taking place. I was a new mom adjusting to having a newborn and now I was grieving. Some days it felt like it was too much to handle. It was at this time in my life I needed my mom the most and she couldn't be there for me. She was in the middle of processing her death, leaving behind her husband, her children, her grandchildren, and now her new grandchild. I felt so many emotions and I had so many thoughts.

I was not only grieving over losing my mom but what my future would be like without her. She wasn't going to see me as a mom. My son wasn't going to know my mom and know her as a grandmother. I will be honest, during this time, I didn't feel like I had an addiction to hope. I was angry with God. I am so glad God can handle our emotions and He understands exactly what we are going through. God didn't reject me for being angry. He didn't stop loving me. He didn't stop pursuing me in my addiction to hope.

My mom passed away when my son was four months old. I began to question everything I believed spiritually. Grief is an interesting process. It has a way of causing people to question life and their own meaning of life. This was a huge turning point for me. It was my addiction to hope that had been established during the panic disorder that prepared me for this major shift in my life. An addiction to hope creates an intimate relationship with God. God is amazing. Through the panic disorder, God developed my addiction to hope creating an intimate relationship with me. Why? God longs to have an intimate relationship with us. He is a God of relationship. When you have an intimate relationship with someone, you are able to go to them and talk about your feelings, bring your questions, share your hurt, express your anger, because it is a safe place. You don't fear they are going to reject you or terminate the relationship because you have already established an intimacy and trust with them. God knew I was going to lose my mom to cancer. He knew the road I was going to walk. Because of my intimate relationship with God, I could be angry with Him. I was able to go to Him with all of my thoughts, my questions, my hurt, and all of my fears. I didn't have to fear He was going to leave me or reject me.

I began to have many conversations with God. I want you to know that when you have a conversation with God,

He will speak back to you. He longs to have a personal relationship with you. God began to show me how I had developed codependent relationships in my life that led to distorted spiritual thinking and unhealthy relationships. It was not only in my personal life but also in my relationships within the church, with church leadership, and at my job. God began to open my eyes to the motives of my heart. This was not an easy process. Be aware, when you begin to ask God questions and ask him to show you things, He will show you, and you may feel uncomfortable.

God also began to heal the wound of the loss of my mom. We have to remember grief is an ongoing process. It takes time to heal. But while I was grieving, I was clinging to God. I had learned how to cling to God during the panic disorder. I knew that's all I could do. It was my addiction to hope that moved me forward. As I moved forward, I drew closer to God. As I drew closer to God, my addiction to hope increased.

I want to make it clear that as you develop an addiction to hope, it does not mean that when you face hard and difficult situations you won't experience thoughts of fear, despair, or even question God. An addiction to hope develops a resiliency within in your spirit and soul so that when you encounter a difficult situation and you feel you have been knocked down for the last time, there is something deep within you that begins to rise above the pain, the fear, and the hopelessness and lifts you back up. This is the hope that only comes from God.

Addiction to Hope is Not Codependency

Now that you have an understanding of what an addiction to hope is and how it is developed, I am going to explain what it is not. I often have clients come into my office feeling frustrated and let down by God because they had believed God for a breakthrough, or a change in their life or a relationship, and it didn't happen. A lack of understanding of what an addiction to hope is can lead to confusion in your relationship with God. The goal of this chapter is to help you decipher between an addiction to hope and unhealthy codependent relationships.

After the loss of my mom, I went through a few years of feeling numb and unsure of my life. The process of grieving exposed the unhealthiness in me and that surrounded me. God strategically used my experience with panic disorder to develop an addiction to hope in me because He knew I was going to need it for the challenges that were ahead. As I went on this quest with God, He began to show me the answers to my questions. God began to identify and show me areas in my life that over time would eventually kill and/or inhibit my addiction to hope.

Distorted beliefs can suppress our addiction to hope because they are attached to a fear. There are several different types of fear people struggle with. I have listed a few of these fears.

- I won't be loved.
- I will never be successful because of how I grew up.
- I'll never overcome this problem in my life.
- I'm too broken.
- God doesn't care that much about me. He has more important things to focus on.
- God will do this for someone else, but not for me.

There are multiple distorted beliefs that develop early in our lives that are birthed out of fear. What God began to show me was that a fear I had created was the distorted belief God did not care about the desires of my heart. This was a fear the enemy was using as an attempt to end my addiction to hope. This fear led to the unhealthy, codependent relationships I found myself in.

What is the difference between an addiction to hope and codependency? Like many people, I would have said I had an addiction to hope during my marriage based on what I thought was an addiction to hope. I was married for twenty-five years. It was not a healthy marriage. I married when I was twenty-one and I did not have enough knowledge to understand fully what a healthy relationship is. I tried to make the best of the marriage. However, I was not aware of my own issues at the time nor my ex-husband's issues.

As the years passed, the marriage continued to deteriorate. I began to read all of the marriage books I could find to see if the authors' suggestions for a healthy marriage would remedy my marital issues. For this to work, it is helpful if both spouses read the book(s), and it is a necessity that both people have a desire to grow in the relationship. I would have said I was addicted to hope, believing this marriage was going to change and that my husband was going to see the light, coming to an awareness of his issues, and our marriage would be saved. Unfortunately, it did not go in that direction.

Feeling hopeless in my marriage, I began to immerse myself in ministry instead of immersing myself in the presence of God. I taught a marriage class at our church, thinking surely that would help my marriage. However, nothing changed. I thought for sure all I was doing for God and for the Kingdom of God was going to bring the answer to my prayers.

What I learned was that I did not have an addiction to hope. I was codependent. So, what is the difference? Codependency can be defined as a person being dependent upon another person to meet a need he/she has, and/or supporting and taking ownership of, and/or enabling someone's destructive behavior instead of allowing natural consequences to occur, and not setting healthy boundaries and putting consequences in place.

In my marriage, instead of confronting and setting healthy boundaries with regard to the emotional neglect and the neglect in other areas of our marriage, I started to take ownership of the marriage problems. I am not saying I did not contribute to the marriage problems. One of my personality traits is conflict avoidance. As with all marriages, there is a negative cycle that each spouse plays a part in. When a spouse does not confront the issues within the marriage, that becomes part of the negative cycle within the marriage. Instead of confronting the issues, I began to believe it must be something I am doing that is causing this rejection and neglect, so I need to change me. I began to put the focus on myself. My codependency enabled my then husband to continue in the destructive behavior that was destroying our marriage and kept me spiraling into negative thoughts and beliefs about myself and God.

Was it unhealthy for me to read marriage books and desire a change in my marriage? No. What was unhealthy is that I took on all of the responsibility for the problems in the marriage and did not openly confront the issues. I had even gone to the extent of bringing God into my codependent plan for my marriage. You might say I was trying to manipulate God to create change in my marriage by immersing myself in ministry and all that I was doing "for God."

I took a book that was very popular at that time on how to pray for your husband and I began to pray religiously using the prayers outlined in this book. That had to be a good thing. Right? Of course, God was going to answer those prayers! Again, that did not work. Does that mean you should not be praying for your husband or wife? Absolutely not! The problem was I went into praying for my husband and my marriage with my own agenda, with my codependency. Was it wrong for me to pray for my marriage to be saved and for my husband to receive deliverance? Absolutely not! I did what so many of us do when we go to prayer. I was not going into prayer seeking God's will and direction for my life. Yes, it is God's desire for all marriages to be healed. However, God will not override a person's freewill. The struggle I had was with my preconceived idea of what the answer to my prayer(s) was going to look like and that was all I was going to accept from God.

It's important to understand that anytime we go to God with our answer to the prayer already in our mind, we shut the door to hear and understand God's answer to our prayer because we are not seeking His will. At times, we become unwilling to accept the answer He gives. This can create bitterness toward God because we assume He is not answering our prayer. We want God to give us the answer we want. The difficulty lies in that we cannot see what God sees. God sees the future. He could see that in my marriage, my then husband was not going to change. God knew what was going to happen. In my human mind, I could not see another possibility for the answer. I did not realize that God was working all things for my good, even in my unhealthy marriage.

My codependency created feelings of hopelessness and despair because nothing was changing, and I couldn't get God to make it happen either. Codependency never brings hope. It brings hopelessness. Codependency and hope cannot go together. It is the opposite of an addiction to hope. Codependency brings about distorted beliefs and thoughts and is based on you fixing the problem or relying on another person to fix the problem and/or meet your need. This never works when it involves other people with their own freewill.

It was during this time, I began to rehearse the belief that God does not care about the desires of my heart, because if He cared about them, He would answer my prayer. I have a distinct memory of the day I took the book on praying for your husband and I tossed it in the trash. I thought, *this doesn't work. God does not care about my desires.* Clearly, that was a lie. But codependency is self-centered. It is focused on what I feel I need and want from the other person.

I was angry at God because He was not answering my prayer the way I thought He should answer. I was doing everything a good Christian would do to have their prayer answered. So I thought. What I didn't realize was that God was answering my prayer. It just didn't look like the answer I thought I was going to get. I began to allow the distorted belief that God does not care about the desires of my heart to take root in my thoughts, and it began to suppress the truth of God's word. It began to limit the addiction to hope that God had already developed within me.

The truth is God does care about the desires of our heart, and He longs to fulfill our desires. God's Word says in Psalm 37:3,4 "Trust in the Lord, and do good; dwell in the land and feed on His faithfulness. Delight yourself also in the Lord, And He shall give you the desires of your heart" (NKJV). I was so focused on verse 4 of this passage as I complained to God that I did not pay attention to the preceding verses. I was not trusting in the Lord. I was not feeding on his faithfulness. And I was not delighting myself in the Lord. You cannot delight in someone you do not trust.

Codependency will blind you to the truth of God's Word, which is necessary to maintain an addiction to hope. It keeps you self-focused and looking to the other person to meet your needs and/or bring you fulfillment instead of looking to God. An addiction to hope puts the focus and trust on God to meet your needs, not a person. An addiction to hope says even though I don't understand what is happening and I'm not seeing the answer I want, I know God has something great for me. I understand, it's hard to do that when everything seems to be crumbling around you. It was hard to understand what God was doing as the years passed, and no change occurred in my marriage. I went through some dark times during those years as God began to break my codependency and began to reignite my addiction to hope.

When does an addiction to hope begin? When you have nothing left to cling to but God. I couldn't cling to my then husband. I couldn't cling to the marriage. I couldn't cling to ministry. All I could do was cling to God. Every evening I would take my dog for a walk, and God and I would have deep conversations. I shared my hurt, my fears, my hopelessness, my raw emotions, and desires. God heard it all. I wasn't seeing an answer, but hope was rising. That's what an addiction to hope does. It goes past your experiences into the very presence of God (Hebrews

6:19). You cannot have an addiction to hope without being closely connected to God. You become dependent on God as your source of hope, peace, joy, and fulfillment.

It was a six-year journey God took me on before my marriage ended in divorce. To many of you, that may seem like a long journey! When I was in the middle of it, it felt like a long journey. However, I would not change those six years for anything. They are precious to me. It was during that time I developed a deeper level of emotional intimacy with God. I began to see and uncover how much God loves me and that He does care about the desires of my heart. Instead of waiting for my then husband to change, I started waiting for God to direct me.

An addiction to hope, unlike codependency, does not rely on a person. It fully relies on God.

Addiction to Hope Is Love

This chapter may be the most significant chapter in this book. It is also the most difficult for me to write. This chapter focuses on the amazing love God has for you. I will be honest; I feel the least qualified to explain how much God loves us since this is an area in my spiritual walk I have struggled with. It is only through God's amazing love for me that I am able to write this book. God has spent my entire life chasing me to show me how much He loves me. It is the deep love of God for you that will cause Him to chase you down and overwhelm you with His love and hope. When you get a deeper understanding of how much God loves you, it will strengthen and fuel your addiction to hope.

If I asked you, "Do you know God loves you?" I imagine most of you would say yes. We all have this intellectual response and knowledge that God loves us. But do you know *how much* God loves you? I was one of those who would always say I know God loves me. However, when God began to challenge areas in my belief system, I found out quickly how much I struggled with truly believing how deep God's unconditional love is for me.

As I mentioned previously, our addiction to hope is tied to our relationship with God because true hope can only come from God. To help you understand my own personal struggle, I am going to share a little of my background.

I grew up in a Christian home. My parents were pastors. I was literally raised in church. Every time there was a church service or event, we were there. I am thankful for my strong spiritual roots. It has been my deep spiritual roots that have kept me in relationship with God. However, there were some legalistic beliefs that became entrenched in my belief system that prevented me from fully accepting and understanding God's love for me. Legalistic beliefs come from a belief system that says I must do something to earn, and/or behave a certain way in order to receive God's love. It is about you obtaining the love of God in order to receive God's love.

I struggled with this fear that I was going to do something that would cause God to reject me. I was always fearing He was going to reject me. At the same time, I was reading the Word of God that says I am to trust in Him and believe He has a deep love for me. Fear cannot be combined with love and trust. You cannot fear someone, trust them, and receive their love. Love brings freedom. Fear brings bondage. You cannot be free and bound at the same time.

You can understand the spiritual conflict I was experiencing. I am confident many of you reading this book can identify with how I was feeling. I believed I was only going to get the blessings of God and the love of God if I was good enough. I felt like I was on this perpetual hamster wheel of trying to please God in order for Him to love me and be able to receive His blessings. If you are struggling in this area, I hope this chapter will help you understand how much God loves you and that you will be able to freely receive His love.

In chapter two, I shared how it was during the panic disorder that God began to develop in me an addiction to hope. A specific memory became etched in my mind during that time. I was driving through my neighborhood one day and I was feeling overwhelmed with the anxiety and fear that I was going to have a panic attack. I began to cry out to God to deliver me from this horrible fear. What struck me about that moment was as I was sobbing and crying out to God, I began to say over and over, "God loves me. God loves me. God loves me." I think it was really the first time it had dawned on me that God *really* loves me. I felt God's presence in my car with me. It felt like God came down in a very dark and hopeless moment and flooded my car with His presence just to let me know He loves me.

God reveals Himself and His love to us during the very dark times in our life. The scriptures tell us He dwells in thick darkness. He is right there with you, no matter how dark it seems. In that moment, I did not come to an immediate revelation of how much God loves me. But it was the beginning of understanding how God has pursued me to show me how much He loves me. God's love pursues each and every one of us throughout our life. The question is, when will you see God's love is chasing you?

The legalistic beliefs were still there. As I mentioned, they were entrenched in my belief system. I wasn't even fully aware of how strong these beliefs were and how much they were affecting my relationship with God. God still loved me, and He still used me in a powerful way. However, I was not able to fully enjoy God's love and the freedom that comes with it. I was still trying to make sure I was doing what I thought I needed to do in order to feel righteous and to feel like I was in good standing with God. This is the contradiction of legalism and the Word of God. God's Word says that our righteousness is as filthy rags (Isaiah 64:6) and that there is no one who is righteous (Romans 3:10). Scripture says that our righteousness comes from God. He is our righteousness (Romans 10:3). Legalism is a person trying to obtain something he/she will never be able to obtain. This is the perpetual hamster wheel. It is exhausting trying to earn something you cannot earn. You cannot earn God's love. It is free.

I'm always amazed at how God works in my life.

Through each difficult time in my life and with the increased development of my addiction to hope, God downloads His love in me. What does that mean? Every time He strengthened my addiction to hope, I became more aware of His love for me. I began to question some of my beliefs. This might create anxiety for some people. I have been there. After my mom died, it scared me when I began to question everything I believed. Though I truly believe it was exactly what God wanted me to do. He wanted to rid me of the distorted beliefs I had about Him.

The journey started with me searching the motives of my heart. I began to question everything I was doing. Why was I doing it? Who was it for? It didn't take long to realize that the majority of what I was doing was not out of my love for God, but out of pleasing others and trying to earn points with God. Something important to understand is that an addiction to hope will draw you out of dysfunction. The very nature of God is that He loves you so much He will pursue you to draw you out of dysfunction and move you into freedom. Every time God was developing the addiction to hope in me, the stronger my connection with Him became. I will be honest, searching the motives of your heart is exhausting work. What does it look like? I will tell you what I did. There was a list of questions I asked myself repeatedly:

Why did I do that?

Why did I say that to that person?

What is my purpose in doing _____?

Why is this important to me?

How does this bring pleasure to God?

What is my purpose in posting this on social media?

I started to notice that a lot of what I was doing was empty works, seeking validation, and trying to make myself appear righteous before others. I challenge you to scroll through your social media, and you will probably discover about yourself some of the same things I discovered. As I started this journey, I also became aware of how judgmental I was toward myself and others. Legalism puts you in the position of a judge, and you judge others and yourself based on works. There is no love in legalism. God's pure love cannot exist in legalistic beliefs. When your belief system is rooted in legalism, it becomes very difficult to love yourself and to love others, much less receive the amazing free gift of God's love.

God began to draw me out of this dysfunctional belief system. He began to expose the lies and bring in the truth of His Word. This was part of the six-year journey I mentioned in chapter three before my marriage ended.

The codependency needed to be broken first in order for me to be able to experience true love. Although, I was still struggling with the spiritual rules and formulas tied to the legalist beliefs I had lived by for so many years. God is an amazing counselor and teacher. He knew the codependency needed to be broken first in order for me to break free from the legalistic thoughts. The legalistic beliefs and codependency are what kept me cycling in the unhealthy marriage and the negative belief system. The legalism led me to be fearful of the judgment of what others and God would say or think of me if I went through a divorce. The codependency kept me trying to figure out how *I* could make the marriage work in order to keep this image of perfection or righteousness. The six-year journey was definitely a cleansing process for me.

Legalism and codependency thrive off of shame. Love and shame cannot coexist. It's either one or the other. Legalism produces shame. It creates thoughts such as:

Why would you do that?

You just can't get it right.

No matter how hard you try you just keep failing.

You'll never be good enough to earn God's love.

You should have known better.

You have made your bed, now you have to lie on it.

You can see how someone might struggle with feeling loved by God when this type of thinking is dominating their thoughts.

People will often ask me how they can make the shift from legalistic thinking to believing in God's love. It starts with changing your thought patterns. Everyone has a pattern of thinking that becomes developed throughout their lifetime, and it is shaped and molded by different experiences. We do not have to be controlled by this thought pattern, however, this pattern can become part of a fixed mindset, making it difficult to change. Our patterns of thinking can keep us in a dysfunctional cycle. One of my favorite scriptures is 2 Corinthians 10:4-6 (ESV):

> For the weapons of our warfare are not of the flesh but have divine power to destroy strongholds. We destroy arguments (one version says casting down imaginations) and every lofty opinion raised against the knowledge of God, and take every thought captive to obey Christ, being ready to punish every disobedience, when your obedience is complete.

There is a war going on over your thought life. Why? Unhealthy thought patterns keep people living in fear, shame, and bondage. When we break the cycle of legalistic thinking, we can move into a place of freedom and acceptance of God's love for us. I often coach others on how to reframe negative thoughts and how to take their own thoughts captive and bring them into the obedience of Christ. Here are a few examples.

Legalistic thought:

I'll never be good enough to get the blessings of God or God's love.

Taking the thought captive to the obedience of Christ:

- Nothing in God's Word says I earn God's blessings or His love. Jeremiah 31:3: God says, "I have loved you with an everlasting love; therefore, I have continued my faithfulness to you."

- 2 Timothy 2:13: "If we are faithless, He remains faithful; He cannot deny Himself."

- Psalm 84:12: God says He gives us "grace and glory," and "no good thing will He withhold from those who walk uprightly."

Legalistic thought:

God blesses other people, but it's just not meant for me.

Taking your thought captive:

- God says He came to give *all* of us life and life abundantly (John 10:10, ESV).

- God says He has great plans for my life; plans to prosper me not to harm me; to give me a hope and a future (Jeremiah 29:11).

I often help individuals get started, then I have them complete the exercise on their own. Did you notice how negative the legalistic thought is? Did you notice when we take the thought captive to the obedience of Christ, it is life-giving?! Love encourages. God's love encourages us. When you take a hold of this concept, it will change your life. It will change your words. It will change your actions. It will develop an addiction to hope.

Hope is born through God's love. When you start truly believing and receiving how much God loves you, hope automatically begins to grow. Oftentimes we view the difficult and hard times in our life as God removing His love from us or punishing us. Life brings difficulties and sorrow to everyone. No one can escape suffering. The good news is God's love shines the brightest when we go through the difficult times!

What does God's love chasing after you look like? It might look different for each person. I think God's love for us is special and unique to the individual. I will share several ways God continues to demonstrate and has demonstrated His love for me. When two people are in love, they will often send little messages to each other with an encouraging word or letting the other person know they are thinking of them. There are many times during my day God will send me a little love note that brings encouragement and hope to me in that moment. Sometimes it comes through one of my social media apps as an encouraging word that pops up with just the right word for my situation. Other times, God will send His love note through an encouraging word from a friend, family member, and sometimes even a stranger! We serve a creative God, and He loves to use his creativity to tell us He loves us.

I have a jar of Dove chocolates on my coffee table at work. Each little Dove chocolate has a special message inside on the wrapper. When I was going through a difficult time in my life, God used those little messages to send me encouragement. The right message at the right time. That is not a coincidence, my friend. It was God sending me a love note.

Music is another way God shows His love for me. I come from a musically talented family, and it is a big part of our lives. Oftentimes, a song will come to mind that speaks to a situation I'm going through and will bring encouragement to me. For example, during one of my difficult times, I woke up on New Year's Day with a phrase from a popular worship song on my mind about how a breakthrough was coming, and through faith I would see a miracle. It reminded me that when God makes a promise to us, He will not go back on His word. That was God loving on me and letting me know that a breakthrough was coming for the situations I have been interceding and praying over.

There are multiple examples of God's love chasing after me. God healed me of migraine headaches when I was twenty-seven years old. He delivered me from panic disorder. God protected me from another professional who came after me to sue me when I started my own business. God has poured His blessings out over my business. There are so many things God has done throughout my life to show me how much He loves me. As David said in Psalm 40:5, "You have multiplied, O Lord my God, your wondrous deeds and your thoughts toward us; none can compare with you! I will proclaim and tell of them, yet they are more than can be told." I encourage you to take a few moments to reflect on your life and where God has demonstrated His love for you.

God reminds you and me that He is there for us, He is thinking of us, He knows what we're going through, and He's taking care of it. I challenge you to start looking and acknowledging the many ways God is showing His love for you. If you don't pay attention, you will miss it. If you focus on the disappointments and the difficulties, you may not see it. An addiction to hope is love because God is hope and He is love. Ephesians 5:2 (MSG) says:

Mostly what God does is love you. Keep

company with him and learn a life of love. Observe how Christ loved us. *His love was not cautious but extravagant. He didn't love in order to get something from us but to give everything of himself to us.* Love like that.

I love this! God's love for you is extravagant! He loves you not to get something from you, but to give everything of Himself to you.

No matter what you are walking through today, God's love for you is still there. No matter how dark it seems, God's love is still there.

The Greatest Battle Over Your Addiction to Hope

In life, there will always be some type of battle over your addiction to hope. However, I believe the greatest battle you will face in your addiction to hope will be over the desires of your heart. In my own personal life, this has been the most difficult battle for my addiction to hope. It was during this battle that I experienced the greatest fear and the most intense feelings of hopelessness.

The desires of your heart are typically something that are developed early in life. It is something you desire and long for. I don't have to sit long with a client before I realize what are the desires of their heart. It usually begins with statements like, "This is something I have wanted since I was a child." "I have always wanted to do [blank]." Or "This has been on my heart for a long time." What are the desires of your heart? What is it that you have been longing for throughout your life?

As I mentioned, the desires of your heart are something you have longed for and desired for many years. It is something you cannot stop longing for. If you don't have it or you don't achieve it, you will feel you have missed something in your life. It may cause an empty feeling when it has not been fulfilled. Some examples of the desires of the heart may include a specific career path, love and companionship, having a child, a ministry endeavor. The marker of the desires of the heart is a deep longing and intense desire. I believe God has placed in each of us the desires of the heart. I believe it is unique to the individual. On the surface, it may sound the same as someone else's desire, but what God has purposed to be birthed out of it for you through that specific desire is unique to the individual.

Too often, we minimize the desires of our heart. It isn't a battle over the surface level of the desires of your heart. It is about the destiny God has for you that lies embedded in the desires of your heart. It is the greater destiny that goes deeper into the desires of your heart and what God has for you that will greatly impact the Kingdom of God. Whether the desires of your heart are love and companionship, or to have a child, or a certain career, or a business venture, the desires of your heart are the conduit for God's greater destiny for your life. You are fighting for your destiny. This is the area in our lives where most people begin to feel hopeless when it is left unmet. The devil knows if you win the battle over the addiction to hope for the desires of your heart, you will be more prepared to fight and to overcome every other battle you face for your addiction to hope, and your addiction to hope will be secured and it will spread to others.

Many of my clients who come in for counseling are usually in the middle of the battle for the desires of their heart. They typically do not come into my office saying, "I need help! I'm in the middle of a battle over the desires of my heart." They usually come in expressing feelings of hopelessness, despair, anxiety, and feelings of emptiness. It isn't until we start uncovering the layers of everything going on in their lives that it becomes evident something is missing. And the something that is missing is something significant. Oftentimes, they are in the middle of a loss of something they felt was the avenue to meeting the desires of their heart. Here is where the greatest battle begins.

The greatest battle begins when we feel we have lost what we thought was going to be the answer to the desires of our heart, or we feel we will never achieve or get the desires of our heart. Feelings of hopelessness begin to rise up. Remember our adversary, Satan, I mentioned in a previous chapter? He is waiting right there, ready to help fill your mind with despair and hopelessness with the thoughts: *I guess it wasn't meant for me. I'll never achieve that dream. God will do it for others, but He won't do it for me.* This type of thinking increases anxiety and fear. Why? Because the desires of your heart are not just something that is in you, but it is a part of you. To think you will never get the desires of your heart feels like a part of you is dying.

I know all too well how this battle takes place. I have been there. I believe there are several weapons used against us during this battle. For me, this battle was very different from the battle I faced for my addiction to hope during the panic disorder, the death of my mom, and going through my divorce. Don't get me wrong. Those were very difficult battles. They prepared me for the greatest battle I would face. The battle for my addiction to hope over the desires of my heart was much more intense and was a psychological, spiritual warfare. I am going to share the weapons Satan used against me and how I was able to conquer this battle. I am sure most of you will be able to relate. You will notice all of the weapons that are used, and that will be used, against you during this battle are based on lies and are centralized in your thought life.

The first weapon that was used against me was the thought and belief "it's [desires of the heart] not for you. It just isn't part of God's plan for your life." When these types of thoughts and beliefs enter your mind, they do not enter in this blatant form that is an obvious lie. The thoughts enter in subtle ways so that you do not take notice that it is a lie. This lie entered my mind during my marriage when I realized it was not going to last. I began to contemplate maybe it [desires of my heart] isn't for me. Once you start contemplating and questioning the possibility of not achieving or obtaining the desires of your heart, it's easy for you to shift to the belief, "I guess it isn't for me." This is when the lie starts to take root and begins to grow. We start looking at how it hasn't happened yet, so it must not be for me.

It is at this time when the beginning seeds of hopelessness begin to sprout. Most people, like me, accept that belief and move on with life, distracting ourselves and ignoring the longing that is still deep within, thinking it will go away. It doesn't. We forget about John 10:10,11 when Jesus says, "The thief does not come except to steal, and to kill, and to destroy. I have come that they may have life, and that they may have it more abundantly. I am the good shepherd." So often, we feel God does not want us to have the desires of our heart. We accept that lie as truth and we stop believing for them. But Jesus says He is the one who has come to give us life and give life abundantly! This lie steals the truth from us. God cares deeply about the desires of your heart. He longs to give them to you. He not only wants to give you the desires of your heart, but He wants to give abundantly!

Once the first lie has been developed, many more begin to make their way into your thought life. The second weapon used against me was the lie, *I messed up my life. I'm not good enough. I don't deserve the desires of my*

65

heart. For others, it might be the lie, *I've made too many mistakes. I'm too messed up.* No matter what the lie is, the longing for the desires of your heart never goes away. This is why there is a constant battle and a struggle with hopelessness.

One thing about the lies, there are no scriptures to back them up. However, we still believe them! That is our humanity. Hebrews 11:6 says, "But without faith it is impossible to please Him, for he who comes to God must believe that He is, and that *He is a rewarder of those who diligently seek Him.*"

It doesn't matter the mistakes I've made. It doesn't matter how good or bad I think I am. All I have to do is believe that He is God. He is who He says He is. And believe that He is a rewarder of those who diligently seek Him. All I have to do is diligently seek Him and He will reward me! Satan wants you and me to believe we are too messed up for God to give us the deep longings of our hearts. He will stop at nothing to try to convince you and me of this. This is why it becomes the greatest battle for your addiction to hope.

The most dangerous and lethal weapon that was used against me in the battle in my addiction to hope for the desires of my heart was the lie, *what if everything you believe about God isn't true? He hasn't come through for you yet.* I'll be honest, this weapon scared me. This lie had come to me before when I had lost my mom to cancer. But this time it was different. It was different because I had developed such a strong addiction to hope that I didn't think anything would rattle me or cause me to question my faith like I had before. I didn't realize that the root of this lie had not been removed. It had sprung up again and in a more fierce way. When you are fighting for your God ordained destiny, it becomes an intense psychological, spiritual battle. The fear is what if my desire never comes to pass? When you start believing it will not come to pass, you begin to have an overwhelming feeling of hopelessness and despair. It is a very dark place.

The answer to fighting this battle seems simple enough. Combat the lies with truth. I completely agree. However, what makes this battle so difficult is the amount of fear behind the lies. These lies have typically been there for years and sometimes decades. Making the shift from lies to a place of hope is a huge battle. If you read the introduction to this book, you caught a glimpse from my journal entries of what this battle can look like.

I am going to share a personal part of my battle. When I finally decided to take on this battle for the desires of my heart, I knew it was not going to be easy. I knew I was going to be battling thoughts and lies that had been there for many years, although I had no idea how hard it was going to be. I had to confront the fears face on. When you accept the belief that something will most likely never happen, you become comfortable with it. You don't like it, but you have adopted it into your belief system, and it becomes an unhealthy companion. You will not be able to win this battle if you do not fight to win. You will get tired. You will feel overwhelmed. You will feel like you just can't do it another day. I have been there. There were many times I cried out to God, saying "I just can't fight anymore."

During this battle, we need to remember that our weapons are not man-made weapons. We have to fight from the spiritual realm. The weapons we use are mighty through God to pull down the strongholds the enemy has set up through lies (2 Corinthians 10:4). The phrase, "to pull down strongholds" is a military phrase. It means to capture and destroy an enemy's fortress. We have to capture and destroy the fortress the enemy has established in our minds.

I encourage you to visualize a fortress in your mind. A fortress has high, thick walls. It is placed in a secure location that would be difficult to reach and hard to overtake. It would be very difficult to penetrate or break through without some type of heavy artillery. When you think about the stronghold of lies established in your mind and in your thoughts, you can imagine the high walls of fear, resentment, and bitterness that have been erected around them. The lies have been protected and guarded by these walls that we have allowed to be built.

How do we capture and destroy these strongholds? In Isaiah 57:19, God says, "I create the fruit of the lips." We have to use the words of our mouth as a weapon against the lies that have been established in our thoughts. Proverbs 18:21 says, "Death and life are in the power of the tongue." We can bring hope and life into us through our words. That verse also says we will bear the consequences of our words. Consequences can be positive or negative. The spoken word has power.

When I work with my clients, I instruct them to speak out loud when they are restructuring their belief system. I want my clients to experience a positive consequence through the words they are speaking. One way I started doing this in my own personal life was to write affirmations using scriptures and putting them in the note section of my phone. I would read, and I still read, these several times a day out loud. What I am doing is speaking hope and life over me and into me and breaking down the walls and the established lies. Below is an example of one of my affirmations.

I thank you, God, that I am blessed, and I am prosperous. I thank you that you are my sun and my shield and that your favor rests upon me and no good thing do you withhold from me. I thank you that your mercy follows after me and I am highly favored by you. God, I praise you that my steps are ordered by you and I follow after you and I hear your voice. I thank you, God, that you   are my rewarder, and you are bringing beautiful and wonderful abundant blessings to my life. I thankyou, God, that you long to bring me the desires of my heart and they are on the way. You will not delay. (Psalm 84:11,12; Psalm 23; Psalm 41; Psalm 37:23; Hebrews 11:6; Ephesians 3:20; Psalm 37:4; Habakkuk 2.)

I encourage you to begin to write out affirmations and speak them daily, multiple times a day, if needed. Our words have power and what you speak over you is what will come to pass. Each of us has many automatic thoughts that go through our mind all throughout our day. You probably do not realize that some of the automatic thoughts you have you are speaking out loud over yourself.

For example, one day as I was getting ready for work, I was feeling hopeless about a situation. I recall saying out loud one of these automatic thoughts, "I don't think this will ever come to pass." In that moment, I just spoke death over my situation! As I mentioned in a previous chapter, one of the homework exercises for my clients is to pay attention to the negative, judgmental words they say to themselves and write them down in a journal or note section of their phone. I then instruct them to rephrase the statement with life-giving words. When I caught myself saying, "I don't think this will ever come to pass," I quickly rephrased it and said, "I am scared this will never come to pass. But I thank you, God, that your Word says you are my rewarder and that you will bring me the desires of my heart." I didn't ignore the fear I felt. But I chose not to focus on the fear. I moved past the fear and declared the truth and hope in God's word. I immediately felt relief and hope. Try it and you will see how your spoken words affect how you feel and how you view your situation.

Another important weapon you will need to use during this battle is the weapon of feeding your soul. Feeding my soul became very crucial and helpful to me in winning this battle. Feeding your soul means to take in, think, and meditate on those things that will bring encouragement, hope, faith, and life. There were many days and nights when I would pull up a sermon by some of my favorite pastors on YouTube or Facebook and fill my soul with the Word of God. I specifically chose pastors I knew who had the gift of spreading hope and encouragement. That is what I needed. When you are feeling hopeless and discouraged, you need to fill your mind and soul with life-giving words.

Feeding your soul also includes reading the Word of God. Hebrews 4:12 says that the Word of God is living, and it is powerful. It can discern our thoughts and the intents of our hearts. When we are breaking down the lies that have been set up in our minds, we need the living Word of God to help discern the lies from the truth. As you read God's word, life comes into you because God is in His Word. You may also feed your soul by reading books like this one. Feeding your soul is all about dwelling on God's faithfulness. It is very easy for discouragement and despair to seep in while in the midst of this battle.

I remember one weekend I was really struggling with thoughts of giving up and feelings of hopelessness. I was not only battling for the desires of my heart, but I was also under a lot of stress in a situation with my son. I remember getting ready for church that Sunday morning and experiencing an overwhelming feeling of heaviness. I mentioned in an earlier chapter how God speaks to me through songs. When I woke up that morning, going through my mind, were the lyrics to a song reminding me that I am an overcomer. The lyrics state that when it seems like it's over, God is holding us, and He reminds us that we are overcomers. God knew the psychological, spiritual battle I was going to face when I woke up that morning and He was sending me a message letting me know that no weapon formed against me was going to prosper and I was an overcomer.

However, in that moment, I did not feel like an overcomer. In fact, as I was getting ready for church, I could not shake the heaviness and despair that was setting in. I felt like I was not going to be able to hold it together. I couldn't call anyone for encouragement, because I knew I would lose it and start crying and I didn't want to ruin my makeup before church. I began to ask God to help me. Another song came into my mind reminding me that God is our rescuer, and in our darkest hour He will come to our rescue. I couldn't get these lyrics out of mind.

When my son and I arrived at church, I began to offer a sacrifice of worship to God. My spirit began to lift. The sermon was exactly what was needed for the situation with my son. My son even knew it. The Bible says in Hebrews chapter 10 that we should not neglect coming together to worship God. There is a spiritual energy that takes place when we meet together with other believers. Attending church and being around other believers is part of feeding your soul. Isolation is a weapon the enemy will use against you to keep you in discouragement.

When we left church, both of our spirits were lifted. The spirit of heaviness that I couldn't shake that morning was gone. As I mentioned in the previous chapter, addiction to hope is love, because God is love. He was talking to me from the time I woke up, letting me know He was there, and He was not going to leave me or let me down.

The final weapon I used in this battle for the desires of my heart was the weapon of rest. This was the hardest weapon for me to learn how to develop and use. I will admit I am not very good at resting. I like to feel like I am doing something to help win the war. Little did I know that resting in God was the most powerful weapon of all. I found out quickly that I had never used this weapon before. You can imagine the anxiety I felt as I was trying to learn how to understand and how to use this weapon. I am one of those people who want to learn something quickly and put it to use. Just to let you know, it did not happen that way.

What does it mean to rest? I have a scripture on my wall in my prayer and piano room. The scripture is Psalm 46:10, "Be still and know that I am God." It sounds simple enough, although it was not simple to me. To rest in God is to know He is the one doing the work, and He is fighting for you. At the beginning of the year, I had determined the phrase I was going to tell myself for the year was "God's got this." It didn't take long for me to realize how much I struggled to believe that God's got this. I was frustrated with myself. I wanted to use this weapon of rest, but I had not developed the skill to use it. I think this is why so often we don't use this weapon of rest. We get frustrated because we haven't developed the skill to use it, so we give up and go back to what we know, striving and fighting.

We all can relate to the frustration of learning something new. When I am frustrated, things will come out of my mouth like, "I can't do this." "Am I ever going to be able to do this?" "This is too hard." Do any of those sound familiar to you?

As I was reading in my Bible one day, I came across the passage in Exodus when Moses and the children of Israel were faced with the Red Sea in front of them and the Egyptians behind them. The children of Israel were scared and started to say how it would have been better if they had stayed in Egypt as slaves instead of dying in the wilderness. Moses encouraged them, saying, "Don't be afraid. Stand firm and watch God do his work of salvation for you today (Exodus 14:13, MSG)." I am very familiar with that scripture. It has always been one of my favorites. This time I felt God was saying to me, stop fighting, don't be afraid, and watch God do His work.

I never paid much attention to the following verse in Exodus 14:14. In the Message Bible, it says, "God will fight the battle for you. And you? You keep your mouths shut!" I laughed when I read this verse. Everyone who personally knows me knows I talk a lot and I like to talk.

To keep my mouth shut is a huge task! I talk out loud to myself all day long. I was being told to do two things that are difficult for me. Rest and be quiet. Those two things require self-discipline. Apparently, that is something else I struggle with. I began to recognize that certain words and things I would say interfered with my ability to rest in God. I stopped myself from speaking out loud everything that would enter into my mind.

I thought I didn't have the skills to use this weapon, but as I started learning how to use this weapon of rest, I realized it combined the skills from the previous weapons I had already used. It's called a transfer of skills. When I am working with my clients, I want to find out what coping skills, as minimal as they may be, they have already been using so we can transfer that skill(s) and ability to a new coping skill. I was able to transfer the skill of speaking God's Word and life over me while I was developing the skill of resting in God. God knows what He is doing. He knows we need to acquire the other skills first before we can acquire the skill of resting in Him.

The first thing I did was change my screen saver on my phone to say, "God's got this." I don't know about you, but I probably look at my phone over a hundred times a day. Every time I pick up my phone, I see the phrase "God's got this." I will then remind myself that I can sit back and know that God is taking care of the desires of my heart, and all He is requiring me to do is to wait on Him and let Him do the work. Rest is really about trusting God to take care of you.

There will be things that will come up that will try to pull you out of a place of rest. The old patterns of thinking will continue to surface, because our mind likes to return to what is familiar. This is why the transfer of skills is so crucial during this time. You will have to continue to feed your soul and speak life over yourself and your situation daily. The battle over the desires of your heart will present the greatest challenge and you will become more skilled as you use the spiritual weapons. I would like to say that once you have acquired all of these skills, you are set for life and every battle you face will be an easy win. Unfortunately, that will not be the case. Life will always present challenges and difficulties in which we will need to utilize and practice these skills.

Oftentimes, my clients feel like they have failed when they slip and don't utilize a certain skill that causes them to regress in their progress. Maybe you have felt the same way. I know I have. But I want to encourage you as I encourage my clients. *Don't give up.* It is in our weakness that God is made strong (2 Corinthians 12, TPT). We are not superheroes immune to difficulties and weariness. We are going to struggle at times. Our dependency is on God, not our own ability.

What you need to know about the weapon of rest is that even when we feel inadequate, we can sit back and know the battle isn't ours. The winning of the battle is not based on my adequacy or inadequacy. If it was, then we would not need God or we would never win the battle. I don't have to be perfect and on top of it. I can actually sit back and say "God's got this" because I don't. When we sit back and watch the salvation of our Lord, that is exactly what you do. Sit back.

You now have your marching orders. It's time to begin fighting the greatest battle for your addiction to hope. You have a God-ordained destiny, and it lies within the desires of your heart. Nothing can take God's plan and destiny from you. You will win this battle! When you do, your addiction to hope will greatly increase.

Breaking Up With Fear: A Must for Maintaining an Addiction to Hope

In this chapter, I will be talking about fear in a way that you may have never thought about. Sometimes a shift in your perspective will change how you approach an issue in your life. As you may have noticed, fear is a common theme that has come up several times throughout this book in your fight for your addiction to hope.

This change in my perspective regarding fear in my own life came about while I was walking through a very difficult time. I felt like everything had been stripped from me and I was trying to find my way back. It felt like all I was doing was crying and grieving with God over things that I felt were lost and a future I thought was gone. I noticed the same fear that I had been struggling with several years prior kept coming back up. I was frustrated with myself that I was not able to move past this fear.

During this time, I ended up getting sick, and I had to spend several days at home. I was stuck at home, forced to face this fear. I was tired of living this way. I was tired of crying. I was tired of grieving. I knew God was calling me to deal with this struggle I had with fear. After waking up from a nap, I had an epiphany. It dawned on me. I am in a coercive control relationship with fear. For the first time, I identified my involvement with fear as a relationship. In the past, I would say I struggled with fear and anxiety. But that was not an accurate descriptor for what fear was in my life. I was living with fear day in and day out. I was cohabitating with it. Fear was in my face every single day. The Holy Spirit began to quicken me on how abusive this relationship with fear had become.

In a coercive control relationship, the abuser's intent is to be able to control their partner so that he/she does not act independently or with autonomy. The abuser's intent is to coerce their partner into an oppressed position in the relationship. This is exactly what fear does. It will isolate you. It will gaslight you and cause you to feel like you are crazy. And it will cause you to have a negative mindset about life, about yourself, and your self-worth. An abusive relationship rarely will start out with full force abuse and control. If it did, the majority of people would recognize it right away before some type of bond or relationship is formed. It starts out in subtle forms. My relationship with fear started when I was a child. As a child, I struggled with separation anxiety. In my teen years and early adulthood, I struggled with little fears here and there. As time went on, I noticed that I was struggling with more fears. Fear became the most prominent in my life when I had the panic disorder.

As I started to dissect my relationship with fear, I began to notice the control fear had in my life. I found that there wasn't a day that didn't go by that I didn't have several fears coming in and stealing my peace. The fear could be related to my relationships, my son, my work, or my finances. It was a constant companion. In order to have a relationship, there has to be communication and conversation. I was having conversations with fear on a regular basis that allowed this coercive control relationship to develop and continue. The more I conversed with fear, the more control it had over me. I found myself feeling confused, and my thoughts became more distorted.

A tactic that fear uses is gaslighting. Gaslighting is a type of psychological manipulation to sow seeds of confusion and gain control by causing someone to question their sanity. Fear will gaslight you, causing you to feel crazy. Here is an example of what one of the conversations looked like for me:

> *Did God really direct you to open up your own business? You don't have a task-oriented personality. How are you going to make this work? Your client load dropped this week. How are you going to make ends meet? What made you think you could make this work?*

You can see how the conversation playing out in my head creates confusion and fear. I knew God had directed my steps to open up my own business. There were divine steps that played out in order for my business to get off the ground and take off. When I stop and look at my business, I can say this was God-ordained, and He has been faithful to me and has never let me down. When you have a relationship with fear and there is a bump in the road, fear immediately comes in and starts to question what you are doing, how you got there, and where you are going. This is one example of how fear would gaslight me. This type of interaction with fear was taking place daily in several different areas.

A relationship with fear will also cause you to isolate from your support system. It will cause you to feel overwhelmed and cause you to believe you do not have the energy to be around other people. You may find yourself withdrawing from relationships and friendships. You may find yourself turning down invitations to do things with others and/or attend functions and events. Fear will convince you that you do not have the energy to give to others or to be around other people. This isolation increases distorted thinking. It convinces you that you need to be alone. This is contrary to how we are created and wired as human beings. Our God is a God of relationship. He created us in His image. He created us to need each other. When we begin to isolate and move away from our support system, it increases anxiety and depression.

I found myself pulling away from friends; I stopped attending events, and I even pulled away from attending church consistently. However, I noticed a pattern that when I would have a conversation with individuals who were addicted to hope in my support system, I walked away feeling encouraged and strengthened. But as I returned to my relationship with fear, I began to pull away again and isolate.

Fear is always going to come at you, but you do not have to have a relationship with it. But I was already in a relationship with fear. I knew I had to break off the relationship. As you are aware, it is very difficult to leave a coercive control relationship. It is more than just saying I'm breaking up with fear. Although, that is the first step. I was sitting at my piano, and I began to tell fear I was breaking up with it. I no longer wanted it in my life. I no longer wanted to be paralyzed by fear. I wanted my life back. I wanted the abundant life Jesus said He came to give us (Matthew 10:10). I knew it was not going to be an easy breakup. Fear had been a part of my life for a very long time and had control in many areas of my life.

One of the first things I had to do was change how I

conversed with fear. I knew I could no longer be a weak victim to its control and manipulation. Breaking patterns in our lives is not as easy as it seems. This is the make-it-or-break-it place for your addiction to hope. I had to learn how to become assertive and forceful with my words.

I had to begin to control the words coming out of my mouth. Every time I felt myself falling prey to the tactics of fear, I had to regroup and begin to speak from a place of victory. Below is an example of what I had to do to take my life back from fear through my words.

I will not allow fear to control my life.

I will get through this situation. God has never failed me.

God will take care of me. He has never let me down.

Fear, shut up! The same spirit that raised Christ from the dead dwells in me

(Romans 8:11).

You have no authority in my life any longer.

This will be something you will have to do daily and multiple times a day. Even though my relationship with fear was dysfunctional and was not serving me, I was used to it. It had become normal. You will have to commit to doing the work. You will slip and fall back into the old pattern. Just get back up. Don't stay down. I tell my clients it's okay to slip and fall. Just get back up and start again.

In the breakup with fear, I knew I had to stop isolating. For me, I slowly moved myself out of isolation. I knew I had to be careful of how I emerged from the isolation. When I am working with clients who are leaving an abusive relationship, I am very strategic in helping them develop a support system and move into relationships that will support healthy behaviors and thinking and that will help guide them moving forward so they do not return to the abusive relationship. I knew I had to start engaging with those who have an addiction to hope so that I would have the support I needed to continue moving out of this relationship with fear. You need to surround yourself with those who will encourage your new freedom. You may not be returning to some of your past relationships. You will need to identify who can support you appropriately. Some of you may need to partner with a professional Christian counselor to help you navigate through your breakup with fear. You may need to join a small group in your church to begin to help feed your soul. It is important to remember you are created for relationship. You need healthy relationships. It is time to stop fear from isolating you.

If you have a relationship with fear, I hope you are ready to break up with it. You can start simply by saying,

"Fear, I'm breaking up with you. I no longer want you in my life. I am no longer willing to give you control over my mind and my thoughts. I refuse to live in bondage to you. God, I thank you for delivering me from fear. I know I will need your help every day in living in the freedom your Son, Jesus, died to give me. In Jesus' name, amen."

Embracing Your Addiction to Hope: Walking in the Confidence That Your Steps Are Ordered by God

Embracing your addiction to hope requires you to understand and accept that our steps are ordered by God. Psalm 37:23 says that the steps of a righteous person are ordered by God. In the second part of verse 23, The New Living Translation states that God "delights in every detail" of our lives. Let me repeat, God delights in every detail of our lives, even the details that are tragic to us.

Walking in the confidence that God orders your steps is not as easy as it sounds. There will be times you will walk through a situation in your life, and you will ask, "Would God really direct this in my life?" When you are in a dark place in your life, it is hard to walk confidently, knowing God orders your steps. There have been many difficult circumstances that I have walked through in life that I questioned God and asked why He would order my steps through these hard places.

One time in particular, I remember feeling confused, disoriented, and grieved over what was taking place. Nothing was making sense. During this battle, there were multiple difficult situations going on in my life. In fact, I felt as if there was no place in my life I could turn to and see or feel calm. During this time, my son was also going through a very difficult time in his life. As a parent, it is heartbreaking to see your child suffer and not be able to do anything about it. At the same time, my business was facing roadblocks at every turn. On top of it, just when I thought the desires of my heart were coming to pass, everything halted. I found myself saying, "Really God? How and why are you ordering this?" I remember when, as a child, I was playing with my sisters and acting silly. I fell really hard, and the wind got knocked out of me. It was a very scary feeling because I felt as if I couldn't breathe, and I was not able to catch my breath. This is how I was feeling mentally, emotionally, and spiritually. I felt as if the wind had been knocked out of me and I couldn't catch my breath. I'm sure many of you can relate.

Questioning God is a tactic the enemy will use to try to destroy our addiction to hope. Our addiction to hope is rooted in the living hope, which is God. If the enemy can cause us to question God, he then can begin to cause us to question our hope. As I began to question God about what was taking place in my life, I found myself losing hope for things to turn around, for the desires of my heart to be fulfilled, and to believe and expect for the very things

I knew God had told me. I began to cycle into a deep depression. When you are close to winning a huge battle in your life, be prepared for intense spiritual warfare. In full disclosure, I felt blindsided. I had seen God move and turn things in my favor over and over, and I was sure the desires of my heart were coming to pass.

Then it happened. Everything turned for what I thought was the worst. In these moments when we feel blindsided, we become the most vulnerable to an attack from the enemy. I felt as if God had betrayed me. I believe God orders my steps. I started to question why God ordered my steps down this path to let me down? I'm sure many of you have felt this way, or you may be feeling this way at this very moment. These thoughts once again opened the door to fear. I felt as if I was back at the beginning of the battle over the desires of my heart. A battle I knew I had conquered. Confusion began to set in. Satan loves to use confusion. When we are weak, discouraged, tired, and weary, it is very easy to become a target of confusion.

To trust that God orders our steps is the most difficult during the most tragic times of our lives. The death of a child. The death of a spouse or parent. A divorce. The loss of your home. A terminal illness or disease. These are the times we usually throw our hands up to God and in desperation ask why He ordered our steps down this path. Many will lose their addiction to hope and walk away from God, believing God has failed them. I hope I can do justice in explaining where God is during these tragic circumstances, and how to trust in the God who orders our steps, and help you maintain your addiction to hope.

As I mentioned, in the midst of tragedy, we begin to question God. When we question God, we begin to turn away from seeing things from a supernatural viewpoint. We begin to focus on the secular realm. The secular realm is what we can see and cannot see taking place around us. It is the world we live in. Our focus becomes our circumstance, and we lose sight of the supernatural power of God.

God does not dwell in the secular. There is no part of God that dwells in the secular. He *moves* in the secular realm, but He operates from the supernatural realm. Everything God does is from a supernatural standpoint. In Isaiah 55:8-10, God says, *"I don't think the way you think. The way you work isn't the way I work." God's Decree. "For as the sky soars high about earth, so the way I work surpasses the way you work, and the way I think is beyond the way you think" (MSG).*

It is easy for us to become confused and disoriented when the steps God orders for us take us down a road where we experience pain, hurt, sorrow, and disappointment. It is easy to become fixated on what we see or do not see in the natural or in the secular realm in which we live. Death, pain, sorrow, evil, and tragedy all take place in our secular world. We are all affected by this world we live in. This is why it is so easy for us to become fixated and stuck in the secular mindset and we struggle to see what we are going through from God's vantage point. No one is going to walk through this secular life without experiencing pain and sorrow. We all share in the brokenness of humanity. But we have a God who says He orders our steps as we walk through this pain, sorrow, and brokenness! And He will delight in every detail. In Isaiah 61, God says He will "comfort all who mourn" and "give them beauty for ashes, the oil of joy for mourning, the garment of praise for the spirit of heaviness."

When God delights in every detail of our lives, it means He is present with you during the dark places. He will not leave you. He will comfort you. He will give you joy in place of mourning. And He will work it *all* for your good (Romans 8:28, NKJV). I know it doesn't feel that way when you are walking through hard times. I had someone ask me one time how the death of their child could possibly work out for their good. I don't have the answer to that question. All I know is that when our lives are subject to the horrors of this world, our heavenly Father is right there with us. He is with you in the pain, the anger, the sadness, the despair, and the ashes. Even when you feel God has left you, He is still right there. He will get you through. I cannot tell you what is on the other side for you. However, I know God will never leave you brokenhearted. Psalm 34 says that God is close to those who are brokenhearted.

Our feelings will often cause us to falter in our addiction to hope. I tell my clients frequently that their feelings are real, but they are not fact. Feelings are just feelings. Our feelings are fluid, and they are subject to change quickly. When you allow your feelings to rule your life, you will live in a constant state of emotional unrest. This emotional unrest will cause you to feel depressed and anxious. It will affect your physical and mental health. Not to mention your spiritual health. When I am walking with my clients through deep grief and loss, I validate their feelings. Many times, our feelings are valid, but we cannot allow them to control us. I understand how difficult that can be when we are walking through deep grief. We have to navigate the delicate balance of allowing ourselves to experience our emotions without dwelling on our emotions. If you are struggling to find the balance, it can be very helpful to work with a good professional Christian counselor. There are times when we need the support and guidance of another person to walk alongside us.

Walking in the confidence that God orders your steps will require you to use the weapon of rest I described in chapter 5. The weapon of rest will allow us to be able to walk confidently knowing that God orders our steps even when we don't understand what is happening. When you can accept and rest in the fact that even through the difficult and hard times, God is ordering your steps, worry, stress, and discouragement over what is or isn't happening will begin to fade. Repeating over and over, "God, I don't understand this. This doesn't make sense," caused great difficulty for me to be able to walk in the confidence that God orders my steps.

The challenge lies in that, as human beings, we have a need for cognitive closure. To simply state, it means we want an answer for what we are going through. It depends on the circumstances as to how obsessed we may become with trying to find an answer. Some people will struggle more with the need for cognitive closure than others. There are tragic things that take place in our lives that do not make sense. Walking in the confidence that God orders my steps means I have to surrender to God my secular and natural mindset and my need for cognitive closure by shifting to a supernatural mindset. There will be things we will walk through that we will receive an answer for quickly, some things we may not have an answer for until years down the road, and still some we may never have an answer for until we reach heaven.

Something we struggle to understand is that God has already gone ahead of us and He has put things in place that help us during the difficult times. What I couldn't see as I was walking through the devastation of my marriage ending, was that God had gone before me preparing the way for me financially, setting up the right people and relationships to start my own business successfully, and to prepare me spiritually and emotionally for the battles I was going to face ahead of me. If you only focus on the circumstance, the tragedy, the grief, the loss, you will not see how the supernatural power of God has already gone ahead of you and prepared things for you and that He will continue to take care of you during the thick darkness.

I cannot see into tomorrow. I cannot see what will happen in the next five years. I cannot see or know what is in someone else's mind and/or thoughts. However, when my mindset moves to the supernatural, my expectations change. I do not have to walk in fear over what has happened or what may not take place. It all goes back to trust. I cannot walk in the confidence that God orders my steps if I do not trust Him to take care of me. When we come to accept that God orders our steps as we are walking through difficulties we did not choose, we will begin to rest in the living hope, knowing that God is carrying us through and that He has a plan and a good outcome for us.

Even when we walk through tragedy due to our own poor choices, if we will submit ourselves to God, He will order our steps to bring something good out of it. Our God is a faithful God who keeps covenant and mercy to those who love him and keep his commandments (Deuteronomy 7:9). He will be faithful to bring you through whatever it is you are walking through today. He is faithful. He cannot deny Himself (Ephesians 2:13). I encourage you today to take a bold step in verbally acknowledging that God is ordering your steps and that you will walk confidently, knowing He is directing you through whatever difficulty or tragedy you are going through today.

Fostering an Addiction to Hope

Once you have developed an addiction to hope, you must learn how to foster it to be able to maintain it. It is very important that you be intentional with surrounding yourself with other hope addicted people who can effectively support you and encourage you. You cannot isolate yourself. Isolation leads to an increase in distorted thoughts and depression, putting your addiction to hope at risk.

I have become very intentional of the people I let into my inner circle. Not every person who is a believer has secured an addiction to hope and may not be capable of supporting and or fostering your addiction to hope. The first rule of thumb is to hang out with those who have an addiction to hope! Proverbs 27:17 says that we are to sharpen one another. That means I need to surround myself with those who are going to encourage me, challenge me to grow, and help me foster my addiction to hope. And I need to be someone who can sharpen others. I love my friends who encourage and challenge me.

We all have had, or some of you may still have, close friends and family who deplete us. You spend time with them, and you walk away feeling exhausted, tired, and negative. In order to foster your addiction to hope, you will have to limit your time with these individuals. The more time you spend with people who do not have an addiction to hope, it will drain your addiction to hope. When you surround yourself with the right group of people, a tribe of hope-addicted people, you will become energized. You will start to speak hope over yourself and others automatically. It is alive. It is full of energy. It is fostered among other hope addicted individuals.

As I discussed in the previous chapters, there will always be something that will contend for your addiction to hope. This is why is it is crucial when you are fostering your addiction to hope, you stay vigilant of the attacks that may come, especially after a recent battle for your addiction to hope. I had come to a point where I was feeling confident about my addiction to hope. I had come off of a really big battle. I was on a high. I had battled hard and God had brought me to a place of rest and I was seeing the results of the win. I hate to admit it but I did not stay vigilant to what could possibly come around the corner. Of course, we cannot see the future and we will not be able to predict what can or may happen. But it is important not to get too comfortable thinking it is all over and there will not be another battle for a long while. Remember, our adversary Satan, hates our addiction to hope.

All it took for me was one little question in my mind

that started with "what if..." He will use the same weapons over and over. He just mixes them up each time he comes against us. Before I knew it, I was back in a battle over my addiction to hope! You have to continue to drill and practice the weapons I mentioned in chapter 5. Fostering an addiction to hope means you are prepared for the next attack. It does not mean you will not struggle hard during the next attack. However, having the weapons and skills handy and ready for use will result in a quicker recovery. You will not stay down and feeling defeated as long as in previous battles. I can say I have been hit pretty hard and even though it gets very difficult, I do not stay down as long as I did in the past. You have the ability to bounce back more quickly. Fostering an addiction to hope will require ongoing practice of the weapons and skills.

You also have to talk from a place of victory in order to foster an addiction to hope. It doesn't matter with whom I am talking; I talk from a place of victory. Defeat is not an option. For me, this is easier to do for others than for myself. Your words will either foster your addiction to hope or cause it to falter. Using the daily affirmations to speak over yourself is a great way to foster your addiction to hope. You will find the more you speak from a place of victory, you will start to speak hope over yourself and others automatically. Our hope is established in God's

Word. To talk from a place of victory, you need to speak the Word of God over your life. My hope is in the promises of God. Speaking from a place of victory will require you to speak His promises. Below is an example of how to speak God's promises over yourself (and others) from a place of victory.

> God, my hope will always be in your promises to me that no weapon formed against me will prosper and every word spoken in judgment against me I will condemn, for this is the heritage I have in you (Isaiah 54:17).

> God, my hope will always be in your promises to me that when the enemy comes in like a flood, You will raise a standard against him and cause him to flee from me (Isaiah 59:19).

> God my hope will always be in your promises to me that You are my rewarder because I diligently seek you and you are bringing beautiful things to pass in my life (Hebrews 11:6).

> God, my hope will always be in your promises to me that no eye has seen and no ear has heard, and neither can the heart of man comprehend the things you have in store for me because I love you (1 Corinthians 2:9).

God, my hope will always be in your promises to me that You are able to do exceedingly, abundantly, above all that I ask or can imagine according to Your power that works in me (Ephesians 3:20).

When we begin to speak God's promises over our lives, hope rises. It will automatically fuel your addiction to hope. Oftentimes during a battle, we will become discouraged and the will to speak God's promises over our lives and situations becomes weak. We will have to fight against discouragement. Discouragement is one of the main tactics the enemy uses to try to destroy your addiction to hope. When you find yourself feeling discouraged, it is important to do what David did when he had become greatly distressed. The Bible says that David encouraged himself in the Lord. When we begin to speak the affirmations using God's Word over our lives, we are encouraging ourselves in the Lord.

Fostering an addiction to hope is an ongoing process. It requires us to continue to speak hope into our lives on a daily basis. I have developed a habit of daily reading hope-filled affirmations over my life, my son's life, and other significant people in my life. I have found that on days I'm feeling somewhat discouraged, after I read my affirmations, I feel encouraged. If you are unsure of how to write out the affirmations for yourself, there are many resources available on how to pray and speak God's Word over your life. One of my favorite books that has helped develop this skill in my life is the book *Prayers that Avail Much* by Germaine Copeland.[2] Today is the day to start fostering your addiction to Hope.

Addiction to Hope Is Contagious

In order to be contagious with hope, you first have to be infected with hope. What does it mean to be infected with hope? One of the definitions of the word infect in the Miriam Webster dictionary is, "to invade (and individual or organ) usually by penetration." To penetrate means to pierce or diffuse into or through something. To diffuse means to pour out and permit or cause to spread freely. When you become infected with hope from God, you will become contagious, and it will pour out of you and spread freely! We are all called to spread hope. Think of a time when someone infected you with God's hope. The infection of hope usually takes place when a person is in a dark place in their life. That is when we become the most susceptible to be infected with hope. Who infected you with hope? Was it a friend, counselor, family member, or a stranger? We all have the ability to infect others with the living hope of God. We all can become contagious with hope!

In each and every one of you lies a story that can be used to help spread hope freely to those around you. Nobody goes through life without experiencing some type of difficulty, hurt, devastation, and despair. It is during the difficult times, God wants to establish in you an addiction to hope so that when you reach the other side, you are able to spread hope to others around you. Your story *is* important. I've seen many people minimize their story or hide their story, not fully realizing how it can help someone else move from a place of despair to a place of hope. Do not be ashamed of where you have been and what you have gone through in your life, whether it was brought on by someone or something else, or through your own choices and decisions. I think sometimes we believe others want to see a polished view of who we are as a person. Or we downplay what we have been through because we think it will cause others to view us as broken or flawed. I have news for you. We are all broken and flawed! I am not perfect. I will share some insight with you as a licensed counselor—we counselors often feel we have to present to others that we have it all together and that our family life and our relationships are great. Well, we don't have it all together.

I was talking with a close friend who is also a counselor who had just walked through a very difficult time in a relationship. My friend shared how embarrassed they felt because of the situation they were in. They also shared how they felt less confident in themselves and their ability as a counselor because of what they had walked through. This was my time to spread my addiction to hope to my friend. How do you spread hope? It is actually very simple. I told my friend even though we are counselors, we are not immune to life's hardships and difficulties. We are counselors, but we cannot predict the future. I shared with this person they are still an incredible, talented, gifted, and a competent therapist. I shared some of my own shame I have experienced in my life and how these hard times will cause us to come out stronger on the other side. I also told this person they have better days ahead of them and they will get through this. I shared with them they are worthy to be loved, cared for, and valued for the person they are.

When we spread hope, we are breathing life into someone who feels like they are dying. It is an amazing thing to breathe life into someone who is dying on the inside. 1 Peter 1:3 says, "According to His great mercy, He has caused us to be born again to a *living hope* through the resurrection of Jesus Christ from the dead." When you are infecting another person with hope, you can actually feel the live hope moving through you! Since it is a living hope, it diffuses and pours out of you into the other person, bringing life into them, and it isn't long before they begin to develop hope. When you breathe life into that person, bringing hope, your addiction to hope also increases.

It is interesting how you will attract people who are going through a difficulty you have already walked through. I do not believe it is a coincidence. I believe in divine appointments. After God brought me through the panic disorder, it was amazing how many people I met who were suffering from anxiety and panic attacks. Nothing is wasted with God. When you go through difficult times and God develops an addiction to hope in you, He will bring others to you who are suffering in the same way you have experienced. The purpose is for you to help them move to freedom and assist them in developing an addiction to hope.

I get excited when I meet someone, or I have a client who comes into my office struggling with anxiety and/or panic attacks. Why? Because I know they can experience freedom! I am able to assist them on their journey to freedom because I have been there. You will experience an energy that will flow through you when you begin to talk to these individuals about what they are going through and how you have walked a similar path. The energy is that living hope that comes through the risen Christ that brings life. Whatever battle you have faced for your addiction to hope, you get to infect and spread hope to others!

Here are some simple steps on how to spread your addiction to hope to others.

Step 1. Find someone who needs to be infected with hope!

Step 2. Share your story. You have to know and believe

that your story is significant and important. What has God brought you through that drew you closer to Him and increased your hope in God? You may have several stories like mine. Have you walked through a divorce? Overcome an addiction? Have you walked through the death of a loved one? Our loss and pain eventually become our story that can lead others to an addiction to hope. If you have never shared your story and you are hesitant to share, I recommend you practice sharing it with someone who is emotionally safe until you feel more confident. My clients often practice sharing their story with me. The more you share your story, the more your addiction to hope increases. Each time you share your story, the living hope inside of you will increase while it is being spread to someone else.

Step 3. Use words that infect others with hope. There are certain things we can say that can automatically bring encouragement and hope to those around us. I have listed a few below to help you get started.

"You will get through this."

"This difficulty will not last forever. I've been there. It has an end."

"You are not alone. I have walked a similar path, and I'm here if you need someone to reach out to."

"This is a storm in your life, and what is up ahead

of you in the future is going to far outweigh what you are walking through now. You have better days ahead of you."

Encourage them by telling them they are loved, cared for, and valued. Your words can begin to bring healing to another person.

Step 4. Commit acts of hope. Send a simple message to someone who is struggling and let them know you are thinking of them, and you are praying for them. Send a card letting them know you care about them. Send a care package with items that are meaningful to that person that will let the person know how much they are valued. Oftentimes we feel forgotten and isolated when we are going through a dark time and having someone reach out with an act of hope can breathe not only hope but life into us.

It is impossible to have an addiction to hope and not infect those around you. The more you share your story you will become more proficient and effective with infecting others with hope. There are many people who need to be infected with hope and your story is the one that will touch someone and infect them with hope. Get your story ready! You are about to infect someone with hope!

Endnotes

1 Graham, Billy. "Start Your New Life With Christ."
Billy Graham Evangelistic Association. 2022.
   https://lp.billygraham.org/find-peace-with-god/

2 Copeland, Germaine. *Prayers That Avail Much.*
Tulsa: Harrison House, 1997.

CPSIA information can be obtained
at www.ICGtesting.com
Printed in the USA
BVHW051921220223
659019BV00011B/106